W9-BGZ-619

TABLE OF CONTENTS

CHAPTER		PAGE #
1	YOUR ASSIGNMENT IS ANY PROBLEM YOU WERE CREATED TO SOLVE ON EARTH.	3
2	WHAT YOU LOVE IS A CLUE TO THE GIFTS AND WISDOM YOU CONTAIN TO COMPLETE YOUR ASSIGNMENT.	5
3	WHAT YOU HATE IS A CLUE TO SOMETHING YOU ARE ASSIGNED TO CORRECT.	9
4	WHAT GRIEVES YOU IS A CLUE TO SOMETHING YOU ARE ASSIGNED TO HEAL.	11
5	IF YOU REBEL AGAINST YOUR ASSIGNMENT, GOD MAY PERMIT PAINFUL EXPERIENCES TO CORRECT YOU.	13
6	YOUR ASSIGNMENT WILL REQUIRE SEASONS OF PREPARATION.	15
7	YOU WILL ONLY SUCCEED WHEN YOUR ASSIGNMENT BECOMES AN OBSESSION.	21

Unless otherwise indicated, all Scripture quotations are taken from the King James Version of the Bible.

Seeds Of Wisdom On Your Assignment
ISBN 1-56394-117-1
Copyright © 2001 by Mike Murdock
All publishing rights belong exclusively to Wisdom International

Published by The Wisdom Center · P. O. Box 99 · Denton, Texas 76202

Printed in the United States of America. All rights reserved under International Copyright Law. Contents and/or cover may not be reproduced in whole or in part in any form without the express written consent of the publisher.

You Will Only Be
Remembered
For Two Things:
The Problems You Solve
Or The Ones You Create.

-MIKE MURDOCK

Copyright © 2001 by Mike Murdock • Wisdom International
The Wisdom Center • P.O. Box 99 • Denton, TX 76202

1

YOUR ASSIGNMENT IS ANY PROBLEM YOU WERE CREATED TO SOLVE ON EARTH.

Creativity Is The Search For Solutions.

Let me illustrate. In large gatherings of the past, speakers could not be heard clearly. So, microphones and public address systems were created. Eyeglasses were created for those who have difficulty seeing.

Problems are the catalysts for *creativity.* When an inventor—whether it is Thomas Edison or whomever—invents something, his creativity is based on an existing problem. He *solves* the problem, and he is *rewarded* accordingly.

Why did you buy your car? Because it solved a transportation problem. Why do you watch the news each evening on television? It solves an information problem. So, every *part* of you has an *Assignment*, a problem to solve. Your eyes have the Assignment of *seeing*. Your ears solve the problem of *hearing*.

That is why God created us. God wanted a *love* relationship. He wanted to be *chosen*, *pursued* and *treasured*. So, He created Adam and Eve.

Adam had a problem. So, God created a solution, Eve. "And the Lord God said, It is not good that the man should be alone; I will make him an help meet for him..." (Gen. 2:18,21-23). Each one of us is a *solution*.

When you open your eyes every morning, you are

looking into an entire world *crammed* with *solutions*. Everything created is a solution...to somebody, somewhere, at some time.

You Are A Solution To Somebody.

You are a reward to someone.

Somebody *needs* you.

Somebody *wants* you.

You are *necessary* to somebody, somewhere... *today*.

You were created for a specific and very special purpose...*to solve a specific problem on earth.*

I call this, *The Assignment* (see Jer. 1:4,5).

God will assist you in *your Assignment*. "For thou shalt go to all that I shall send thee, and whatsoever I command thee thou shalt speak. Be not afraid of their faces: for I am with thee to deliver thee, saith the Lord" (Jer. 1:7,8).

It Is Essential That You Discover Your Assignment And Give Yourself Totally To It. "Let every man abide in the same calling wherein he was called" (1 Cor. 7:20).

Everything was created to bring pleasure to God. "Thou art worthy, O Lord, to receive glory and honour and power: for Thou has created all things, and for Thy pleasure they are and were created" (Rev. 4:11).

Your Assignment Is To Solve Problems For Those To Whom You Are Sent.

Remember: *Your Assignment Is Any Problem You Were Created To Solve On Earth.*

2

WHAT YOU LOVE IS A CLUE TO THE GIFTS AND WISDOM YOU CONTAIN TO COMPLETE YOUR ASSIGNMENT.

Love Is The Map To Your Wisdom.

When you have a love for children, a special Wisdom begins to grow and develop in you for children. You begin to understand their fears, tears and desires. When you have a love for animals, you develop an intuition, a special Wisdom for their behavior and conduct. You can sense what they are feeling. When you need Wisdom in your marriage, love for your mate must be birthed first.

Wisdom Is The Product Of Love.

Love Births Persistence. When you love something, you give birth to extraordinary tenacity, determination and persistence. Recently, I read a powerful story about a runner. In his youth, he had a terrible disease. Doctors insisted he would never be able to even walk again. But, something powerful was already within him...his love for running.

His love for running birthed *determination*. He ended up winning a gold medal in the Olympics.

Love is stronger than sickness. It is stronger than disease. It is stronger than poverty.

Find what you truly love, and *build your daily agenda around it.*

You contain certain qualities, special gifts and worthy traits. They make you *unique*. You are distinct from the herd. What is it? What do you *love to talk* about the *most*? *Think* about most?

I discussed this with my staff recently. "If every human on earth was paid $10 an hour for work, regardless of the type of job, what would you choose to do? For example, if you chose to be a janitor of a building, you would receive $10 an hour for it. If you decided that you wanted to be a heart surgeon, you would still receive $10 an hour. What would you love to do if money was not involved?" *That Is Your Life Assignment.*

Moses loved people. When he saw an Egyptian beating a fellow Israelite, he moved quickly. In his passion for justice he killed the Egyptian. That was unfortunate. It postponed his Assignment. But his love for his people was a clue to his mantle as a Deliverer. He was attentive to their *cries*. *He cared*. His compassion ran deep. Because he had a love for people, he was able to lead people.

Abraham loved peace. He despised conflict. So when God decided to destroy Sodom and Gomorrah, Abraham became an intercessor and mediator for Lot, his nephew, who lived in Sodom. His love for peace and justice was rewarded by God. Though Sodom and Gomorrah were destroyed, Lot and his daughters were brought out safely. It happened because Abraham contained something very precious: a love for peace. *His love for peace birthed the Wisdom necessary to achieve it.*

Recently, a close friend of mine came to our ministry and gave a special teaching. He gave us a personality profile that enabled us to discover the greatest gifts within us. He showed us how to examine the lives of Bible characters and how to relate to them. This is one of the most important things you can do. You must find what you really care about and develop your life around it.

It is wise to correct the flaws within you.

It is even wiser to acknowledge and embrace your dominant gifts and expertise.

Permit the *true you* to emerge. I have often heard people insist to a shy person, "You must talk more!" Then the same person will turn to someone talking a lot and say, "Be quiet! Just sit and listen!"

We instruct youth, "Get more serious about life."

We instruct the elderly, "You need to be less serious!"

Do not move away from the essence of what God made you. Understand the importance of your *uniqueness.* Your distinctions must be discovered, embraced and celebrated.

Sameness Creates Comfort.

Difference Creates Reward.

Discern your gifts. *Identify* your difference. Build your daily agenda around it. Whatever you are *gifted* to do is what you should be doing.

Remember: *What You Love Is A Clue To The Gifts And Wisdom You Contain To Complete Your Assignment.*

You Can
Only Conquer
Something
You Hate.

-MIKE MURDOCK

Copyright © 2001 by Mike Murdock • Wisdom International
The Wisdom Center • P.O. Box 99 • Denton, TX 76202

3

WHAT YOU HATE IS A CLUE TO SOMETHING YOU ARE ASSIGNED TO CORRECT.

Anger Is Passion.

It simply requires *appropriate focus*. Have you ever wondered why others were not angry about situations that infuriated *you?* Of course you have.

Anger is a clue to your Assignment.

Moses hated slavery. When he saw an Egyptian beating an Israelite, fury arose. Why? He was a Deliverer.

Three Wisdom Keys In Understanding Anger

- ▶ You Cannot Correct What You Are Unwilling To Confront.
- ▶ Anything Permitted Will Increase.
- ▶ What You Can Tolerate You Cannot Change.

I love Wisdom.

I hate ignorance. I have attended seminars where Scriptures were misquoted, truth was distorted, and error was dominant. It was almost impossible to sit and permit it to be spoken without my open confrontation to it.

You cannot really change or correct something unless you have a God-given hatred for it, whether it is sickness, injustice, racial prejudice, poverty, divorce, or abortion. My friend, Pastor Mike Hayes, calls it, "a Holy Hatred."

Many things are wrong in this country, but they will never be changed until *someone is angry enough* about it to step forward and take charge.

For instance, abortion has slowly become accepted, although it is a truly devastating blight on the moral landscape of this country. It appears that no true and articulate spokesperson has yet emerged who is capable of turning the tide. I thank God for those who are making significant efforts to do so!

The Persuaded Become The Persuasive.

I have asked God often to raise up someone with a burning desire who can *successfully* plead the case of the unborn child. I have asked God to provide a militant, intellectual, passionate zealot who will link the Word of God with the gift of life in my generation —someone passionate and on fire.

That someone could be you.

I am not justifying the bombing of abortion clinics. That is as hypocritical as the abortionist.

I am speaking of *an anointing*, a mantle, a calling when someone *rises up* to complete their Assignment in this generation: to uproot the Seeds of rebellion growing in us.

Your anger is important. Very important. It simply needs an appropriate focus.

Do not ignore it. Satan dreads your fury.

An angry man is an awakened man. Only an angry man can change the mind of the unconcerned.

Anger alone cures apathy.

Focused Fury Is The Key To Change.

Remember: *What You Hate Is A Clue To Something You Are Assigned To Correct.*

4

WHAT GRIEVES YOU IS A CLUE TO SOMETHING YOU ARE ASSIGNED TO HEAL.

Tears Talk.

Whatever makes you *weep* is a clue to something you were created to heal.

Compassion Is A Signpost.

What grieves you? Battered wives? Abused or molested children? Ignorance? Disease? Poverty? Pornography? Homosexuality? Abortion? Identify it. Be honest with yourself.

Caring qualifies you as an *Instrument of Healing.*

What makes you cry is a clue to a problem God has anointed you to change, conquer and heal. Remember Nehemiah? His heart was broken about the walls of Jerusalem needing repair. He could not sleep. He wept long hours.

He was stirred to write letters, contact officials, and even change his personal life to rebuild the walls.

Examine Ezra. His heart was distressed over the temple in Jerusalem. He could not rest. He wept. He knew what few knew.

The presence of God is the only cure for wounded people. He recognized that places mattered and that God would honor and reward those who sanctified a worship center in the city.

Feelings Are Often Signposts To Your Assignment.

Social insanity is epidemic. Observe how the liquor industry has their signs on every billboard of a stadium. Every newspaper contains liquor advertisements. Yet alcohol has killed more people on our highways than those killed in the entire Vietnam Conflict.

Someone said we have lost more of our children to death by alcoholism than deaths in all the major wars. Yet everyone screams about the horrors of war while sipping their alcohol at a cocktail table.

Your Greatest Enemy Is Always Within You.

Someday, God is going to raise up another Billy Sunday or someone who is sickened at the children's brains splattered on a highway. Someone is going to be so grieved over senseless deaths that their Assignment becomes clear. That Assignment will *become their obsession.* Then, they will rise up to launch a war...a holy war that will salvage the lives of thousands and *heal the broken* in this generation.

Have you wept long hours over financial bankruptcy and debt? Think of the many families in America who lack finances because of a father's drinking habit. Think of the children who cannot be put through school because money is wasted on alcohol. Do you weep when you see homeless children?

Tears Are Clues To Where God Will Use You Most.

Oh, there are many things that should set us on fire. What *grieves* you? What *saddens* you? What *moves you* to tears? Pay attention to it.

Remember: *What Grieves You Is A Clue To Something You Are Assigned To Heal.*

5

IF YOU REBEL AGAINST YOUR ASSIGNMENT, GOD MAY PERMIT PAINFUL EXPERIENCES TO CORRECT YOU.

God Cannot Be Ignored Without A Consequence.

God can create painful experiences and unforgettable experiences.

Jonah is a perfect example. He rebelled against God's instructions to, "Arise, go to Nineveh, that great city, and cry against it; for their wickedness is come up before Me. But Jonah rose up to flee unto Tarshish from the presence of the Lord, and went down to Joppa; and he found a ship going to Tarshish: so he paid the fare thereof, and went down into it, to go with them unto Tarshish from the presence of the Lord. But the Lord sent out a great wind into the sea, and there was a mighty tempest in the sea, so that the ship was like to be broken" (Jonah 1:2-4).

Jonah had to endure three miserable days and nights in the belly of the fish before he *accepted* his Assignment.

Never Misjudge God.

He never ignores tiny acts of defiance.

Examine the life of Joshua. When Achan rebelled and kept some of the spoils of war, they lost the first battle of Ai. In a single day, their reputation was stained. Joshua's men lost total confidence. Achan had ignored the command of God. Consequently, the entire nation suffered defeat until obedience became their priority again.

The Disobedience Of One Can Create Corporate Judgment On Many. When one defies the will of God, everyone involved *must pay the price for it.*

A well-known leader said God spoke to him when finances became difficult for his ministry. "Someone on your staff does not belong." He fired the staff member. The finances flowed again. *When Wrong People Leave Your Life, Wrong Things Stop Happening.*

Pain Is Corrective. It happens often in The Potter's House, where our Father is remolding *common clay vessels for uncommon exploits.* "It is good for me that I have been afflicted; that I might learn Thy statutes" (Ps. 119:71).

The Waves Of Yesterday's Disobedience Will Splash On The Shores Of Today For A Season. If you are walking in contradiction to God's laws, expect painful experiences on the road ahead.

Don't waste these Hurting Seasons.

That's where the healing process begins.

6 Rewards Of Pain

1. Pain forces you to *look...*
   ...to the Word of God for answers.
2. Pain forces you to *lean...*
   ...on the arm of God, instead of men.
3. Pain forces you to *learn...*
   ...where you went astray.
4. Pain forces you to *long...*
   ...for His presence and healing.
5. Pain forces you to *listen...*
   ...for changes in God's instructions.
6. Pain forces you to *love...*
   ...whatever remains.

Remember: *If You Rebel Against Your Assignment, God May Permit Painful Experiences To Correct You.*

6

YOUR ASSIGNMENT WILL REQUIRE SEASONS OF PREPARATION.

You Are Not Born Qualified—You Become Qualified.

Moses required preparation. He spent his first 40 years learning the Wisdom of the Egyptians. "And Moses was learned in all the Wisdom of the Egyptians, and was mighty in words and in deeds. And when he was full forty years old, it came into his heart to visit his brethren the children of Israel" (Acts 7:22,23).

He spent another 40 years learning the lessons of leadership and priesthood. "Now Moses kept the flock of Jethro his father in law, the priest of Midian: and he led the flock to the backside of the desert, and came to the mountain of God, even to Horeb" (Ex. 3:1).

"And when forty years were expired, there appeared to him in the wilderness of mount Sina an angel of the Lord in a flame of fire in a bush. When Moses saw it, he wondered at the sight: and as he drew near to behold it, the voice of the Lord came unto him" (Acts 7:30,31).

Moses was a protégé for 80 years.

His first 40 years educated him about *enemy*. His second 40 years educated him about *people.*

Preparation. *Preparation.* PREPARATION.

Jesus required preparation. Jesus spent 30 years preparing for His ministry. "And Jesus Himself began to be about thirty years of age" (Lk. 3:23). These days seem so different for young ministers. The average young minister wants to prepare for three and a half years for 30 years of public ministry. Jesus did the opposite. *He prepared for 30 years for a public ministry of three and a half years.*

The Apostle Paul required preparation. He was a Pharisee and the son of a Pharisee (see Acts 23:6). He had invested years of preparation for the intelligentsia of his generation. "If any other man thinketh that he hath whereof he might trust in the flesh, I more: circumcised the eighth day, of the stock of Israel, of the tribe of Benjamin, an Hebrew of the Hebrews; as touching the law, a Pharisee; Concerning zeal, persecuting the church; touching the righteousness which is in the law, blameless" (Phil. 3:4-6).

The 11 Seasons Of Preparation For Your Assignment

1. Seasons of *Affliction*—"but be thou partaker of the afflictions of the gospel according to the power of God" (2 Tim.1:8). "It is good for me that I have been afflicted; that I might learn Thy statutes" (Ps. 119:71).

2. Seasons of *Chastening*—"For whom the Lord loveth He chasteneth, and scourgeth every son whom He receiveth. Now no chastening for the present seemeth to be joyous, but grievous: nevertheless afterward it yieldeth the peaceable fruit of righteousness unto them which are exercised thereby" (Heb. 12:6,11).

3. Seasons of *Contention*—"But foolish and unlearned questions avoid, knowing that they do gender strifes. And the servant of the Lord must not strive; but be gentle unto all men, apt to teach, patient" (2 Tim. 2:23,24).

4. Seasons of *Credibility*—"But watch thou in all things, endure afflictions, do the work of an evangelist, make full proof of thy ministry" (2 Tim. 4:5).

5. Seasons of *Disappointment*—"For Demas hath forsaken me, having loved this present world, and is departed unto Thessalonica" (2 Tim. 4:10).

6. Seasons of *Injustice*—"Alexander the coppersmith did me much evil: the Lord reward him according to his works" (2 Tim. 4:14).

7. Seasons of *Isolation*—"At my first answer no man stood with me, but all man forsook me: I pray God that it may not be laid to their charge" (2 Tim. 4:16).

8. Seasons of *Persecution*—"Persecutions, afflictions, which came unto me...what persecutions I endured: but out of them all the Lord delivered me. Yea, and all that will live godly in Christ Jesus shall suffer persecution" (2 Tim. 3:11,12).

9. Seasons of *Solitude*—"Greatly desiring to see thee, being mindful of thy tears, that I may be filled with joy" (2 Tim. 1:4).

10. Seasons of *Suffering*—"If we suffer, we shall also reign with Him: if we deny Him, He also will deny us" (2 Tim. 2:12).

11. Seasons of *Warfare*—"Thou therefore endure hardness, as a good soldier of Jesus Christ. No man that warreth entangleth himself with the affairs of this life; that he may please Him Who hath chosen him to be a soldier" (2 Tim. 2:3,4).

As I review the first half century of my life, I can distinguish the seasons. In each season, I felt ignorant and unaware of the *purpose* of that specific season. I wondered, "How could God get any glory out of this situation?" Today, I see His Divine Design.

Did you ever see "The Karate Kid?" It contains

some powerful lessons. In the story, the young boy desperately wanted to learn the art of fighting. His old mentor waited, and instead handed him a paint brush and instructed him to paint the fence. The young man was disheartened, but he followed the instructions of his mentor.

Discouraged, disillusioned and very disappointed, he could not see any relationship between painting the fence and fighting in the ring. When he finished, he was instructed to wash, wax and polish the car. As he moved his hands in a circular motion over the car, he was very demoralized. His thoughts were, "How will this help me in my future? How will this help me achieve my desire to be a great fighter?"

But the old mentor was secretly preparing each motion of his hands to *develop the movements of a fighter.* The young man did not discern it until much later.

Your Heavenly Father Knows What He Is Doing With Your Life. "But He knoweth the way that I take: when He hath tried me, I shall come forth as gold" (Job 23:10).

Some Seasons You May Not Understand His Workings. "Behold, I go forward, but He is not there; and backward, but I cannot perceive Him: On the left hand, where He doth work, but I cannot behold Him: He hideth Himself on the right hand, that I cannot see Him" (Job 23:8,9).

Embrace The Present Season God Has Scheduled In Your Life. Extract every possible benefit. "Wherefore lift up the hands which hang down, and the feeble knees" (Heb. 12:12).

You Will Survive The Fires Of The Furnace. "Though I walk in the midst of trouble, Thou wilt revive me: Thou shalt stretch forth Thine hand against the wrath of mine enemies, and Thy right hand shall save me" (Ps. 138:7).

Seasons Perfect You For Your Assignment. "The Lord will perfect that which concerneth me" (Ps. 138:8).

Success Is Inevitable For the Prepared.

Remember: *Your Assignment Will Require Seasons Of Preparation.*

The Only Reason
Men Fail Is
Broken Focus.

-MIKE MURDOCK

Copyright © 2001 by Mike Murdock • Wisdom International
The Wisdom Center • P.O. Box 99 • Denton, TX 76202

7

YOU WILL ONLY SUCCEED WHEN YOUR ASSIGNMENT BECOMES AN OBSESSION.

Focus Is Magnetic.

When you focus your attention and time to achieving your Assignment, you will experience Favor.

Jesus Rebuked Those Who Broke His Focus. "But when He had turned about and looked on His disciples, He rebuked Peter, saying, Get thee behind Me, satan: for thou savourest not the things that be of God, but the things that be of men" (Mk. 8:33).

The Apostle Paul Was Obsessed With His Assignment. It explains his remarkable victories over enemies, adversaries and even friends who misunderstood him. He explained his focus to the Philippians, "this one thing I do, forgetting those things which are behind, and reaching forth unto those things which are before, I press toward the mark for the prize of the high calling of God in Christ Jesus" (Phil. 3:13,14).

He moved *away* from past hurts, failures and memories. Obviously, he had a *photograph* of those things God had placed before him.

6 Keys For Developing An Obsession For Your Assignment

1. *Identify Any Distraction To Your Assignment.*

"...let us lay aside every weight, and the sin which doth so easily beset us, and let us run with patience the race that is set before us" (Heb. 12:1).

2. *Be Ruthless In Refusing Any Responsibilities Unrelated To Your Assignment.* "No man that warreth entangleth himself with the affairs of this life; that he may please Him Who hath chosen him to be a soldier" (2 Tim. 2:4).

3. *Become An Expert On Your Assignment.* "Study to shew thyself approved unto God, a workman that needeth not to be ashamed, rightly dividing the word of truth" (2 Tim. 2:15).

4. *Avoid Any Conversation With Those Who Disrespect Your Assignment.* "But shun profane and vain babblings: for they will increase unto more ungodliness. But foolish and unlearned questions avoid, knowing that they do gender strifes" (2 Tim. 2:16,23).

5. *Prepare For Uncommon Adversity.* Satan dreads the *completion* of your Assignment. Each act of obedience can destroy a thousand satanic plans and desires.

6. *Disconnect From Any Relationship That Does Not Celebrate Your Obsession.* "And if any man obey not our word by this epistle, note that man, and have no company with him, that he may be ashamed" (2 Thes. 3:14).

I must share with you a personal experience because I am certain it will happen to you in your future (if it has not already happened). My secretary handed me the telephone number of a friend I had known 25 years ago. He had not written me for 25 years. He had not telephoned me for 25 years. He had not sown a Seed in my ministry for 25 years.

Suddenly, he telephoned several times. He came to my weekly Bible study. He sowed a generous Seed in my ministry. He wanted to have a meal together. I consented.

"Mike, I am making more than $20,000 a month. It is the most wonderful company I have ever been involved with. I want you to become a part of it with me."

"Well," I replied slowly, "I am very consumed with my ministry. I really do not have the time to develop a secondary income at this point in my life. But, I appreciate it."

He was stunned. "But I know that you will need a strong financial base when you retire in the future. It is easy. You know thousands of people. You do not have to do anything but ask me to come and present this multi-level marketing plan to your people. They will come because they know you personally. And, this product is the best on the market. People will always need this product. Your people *need* them."

Well, I was impressed with his $20,000 monthly income, but I had to be very direct with him. "I like your product. I believe everyone should have one. I will buy one from you. I will tell my friends about you, but I cannot get involved in selling them, because this product cannot consume my attention, efforts and time. It would be impossible for me to develop an obsession with this product. You see, I know that *I can only succeed with something that consumes me.* Besides that, I have not had an instruction from the Lord to pursue a business with this product."

My instructions had already arrived. *My inner peace was proof I was in the center of my Assignment.*

There will always be others with wonderful ideas

who offer you options to your Assignment. Any hours you spend with them is a waste of their time and yours.

I have never heard from this man since.

You see, he had no interest in my Assignment whatsoever. He was only interested in my involvement *with his dream.* I was merely *a vehicle to generate finances* back into his own life.

My secretary handed me another telephone message recently. It was from a dear friend well known in ministry circles. He had built an incredible work for God, but due to extreme adversity had experienced some major losses in his personal life and in his ministry. I returned the telephone call.

"Mike, we have got to get together soon."

"Great! When do you want to meet?"

"Could you meet me tonight?" was his reply.

I could not imagine why this man wanted to meet with me so urgently. He had not telephoned me twice in the previous eight years. Suddenly, it was life and death. We met and talked. He was involved in a multi-level marketing program. He would succeed and I knew that. I also realized that anyone linked to him would have significant success. He is a remarkable, brilliant and enjoyable friend.

But he had a *different focus.*

I was very direct. "I really believe you could succeed significantly in this business. But, do you feel that this would distract you from the calling of God for ministry?'

"Oh, I will continue to have my ministry, but this will help people financially everywhere."

I replied, "My obsession is the Holy Spirit and spending time in The Secret Place. I have known more peace and joy since building my days around His presence than I have ever known in my lifetime. Wealth is wonderful. But doing the will of God and being in the center of my Assignment is my obsession," I replied carefully.

I have not heard from him again.

When You Make Your Assignment Your Obsession, Wrong Relationships Will Die. Right relationships will be born. The best way to disconnect from wrong people is to become obsessed with doing the right thing.

When Your Obsession Is To Do The Right Thing, Wrong People Will Find You Unbearable.

Fight For Your Focus.

Battle hard. Build walls that guarantee your concentration. Ignore the jeers, laughter and criticism that you are "obsessed."

Only The Obsessed Succeed.

Remember: *You Will Only Succeed When Your Assignment Becomes An Obsession.*

My Closing Thought

If this Wisdom Book has blessed you, I'd love to hear from you! You may order additional copies for a friend, cell group, or associates at your workplace.

The Greatest Gift Of All...Is The Gift Of Wisdom.

Quantity Price List For
Seeds Of Wisdom On Your Assignment (B-122)

Quantity	Cost each	Discount	Quantity	Cost each	Discount
1-9 =	$5.00 ea.	None	500-999 =	$3.00 ea.	40%
10-99 =	$4.00 ea.	20%	1000-up =	$2.50 ea.	50%
100-499 =	$3.50 ea.	30%	5000-up =	$2.00 ea.	60%

(Add 10% shipping all single titles.)

Recommended Books And Tapes:

"The Assignment: The Dream & The Destiny," Vol. 1 *(B-74/$10)*

"The Assignment: The Anointing & The Adversity," Vol. 2 *(B-75/$10)*

"The Assignment: The Trials & The Triumphs," Vol. 3 *(B-97/$10)*

"The Assignment: The Pain & The Passion," Vol. 4 *(B-98/$10)*

"The Leadership Secrets Of Jesus" *(B-91/$10)*

"The Law Of Recognition" *(B-114/$10)*

"Wisdom For Winning" *(B-01/$10)*

"The Assignment," 6-Tape Series *(TS-22/$30)*

Order Your *FREE* Wisdom Gift Catalog!

THE WISDOM CENTER
P. O. BOX 99
DENTON, TX 76202
1-888-WISDOM-1
(1-888-947-3661)
FAX: 940-891-4500
www.thewisdomcenter.cc

Dear Friend,

You matter to me.

You are important to God. If you need special prayer, don't hesitate to write me today.

My staff and I will pray for you and will write you back to help you receive The Answer you desire from God.

God has brought us together for a reason. Will you become my Monthly Faith Partner?

Your Seeds will bless so many....and birth uncommon increase in your own life.

When you sow, expect Four Scriptural Harvests:

- Uncommon Protection (Mal. 3:10,11)
- Uncommon Favor (Lk. 6:38)
- Uncommon Health (Isa. 58:8)
- Uncommon Financial Ideas (Deut. 8:18)

An Uncommon Seed Always Creates An Uncommon Harvest (Mk. 10:28-30).

Pursuing His Wisdom,

Mike Murdock

DECISION

Will You Accept Jesus As Your Personal Savior Today?

The Bible says, "That if thou shalt confess with thy mouth the Lord Jesus, and shalt believe in thine heart that God hath raised Him from the dead, thou shalt be saved" (Rom. 10:9).

Pray this prayer from your heart today!

"Dear Jesus, I believe that you died for me and rose again on the third day. I confess I am a sinner...I need Your love and forgiveness...Come into my heart. Forgive my sins. I receive Your eternal life. Confirm Your love by giving me peace, joy and supernatural love for others. Amen."

Clip and Mail

DR. MIKE MURDOCK

is in tremendous demand as one of the most dynamic speakers in America today.

More than 14,000 audiences in 38 countries have attended his meetings and seminars. Hundreds of invitations come to him from churches, colleges, and business corporations. He is a noted author of over 115 books, including the best sellers, *"The Leadership Secrets of Jesus"* and *"Secrets of the Richest Man Who Ever Lived."* Thousands view his weekly television program, *"Wisdom Keys with Mike Murdock."* Many have attended his annual School of Wisdom at his headquarters, *The Wisdom Center,* in Denton, Texas.

☐ Yes, Mike! I made a decision to accept Christ as my personal Savior today. Please send me my free gift of your book, *"31 Keys to a New Beginning"* to help me with my new life in Christ. *(B48)*

NAME BIRTHDATE

ADDRESS

CITY STATE ZIP

PHONE E-MAIL *YA01*

Mail form to:

The Wisdom Center *· P. O. Box 99 · Denton, TX 76202*
Phone: 940-891-1400 · Fax: 940-891-4500 · www.thewisdomcenter.cc

Your Search Is Over.

- 9 Keys In Making Your Time Count
- 4 Rewards of Pain
- 14 Seasons In A Minister's Life
- 15 Rewards For Completing Your Assignment
- The Benefits of Crisis
- 12 Keys That Unlock The Flow Of Miracles
- 7 Important Keys In Planning
- Importance Of Anger

Everything that God created was created to solve a problem. The key to successful living is discovering the purpose for which you were created. This is your "Assignment." This Volume I on "The Dream & The Destiny" will unleash in you the discovery of our life calling. You will begin to know the joy of being in the center of God's will for your life!

Wisdom Is The Principal Thing
Book / $10 B-74
ALSO AVAILABLE:
6 Audio Tapes / $30 TS-22
The Wisdom Center

Available also on six tapes for only $30!

ORDER TODAY!
www.thewisdomcenter.cc

1-888-WISDOM-1
(1-888-947-3661)

THE WISDOM CENTER • P.O. Box 99 • Denton, Texas 76202

YOU WILL NEVER BE THE SAME

The School Of Wisdom Collection

Wisdom Is The Principal Thing
Four Volumes TS PAK-001 / $99
(A $120 Value!)
Six Audio Tapes $30 Each Volume
The Wisdom Center

Thousands are being mentored through these life-changing Conference tapes. Dr. Mike Murdock deals with many topics including the Holy Spirit, Financial Breakthrough, Time Management Techniques, Goal Setting, Negotiation, People Pressure, Focus, The Law of Order, Unleashing Favor and many more.

- The Uncommon Life (TS-85)
- 101 Wisdom Keys That Have Changed My Life (TS-90)
- What I'd Do Differently If I Could Begin My Life Over Again (TS-83)
- Unleashing Uncommon Favor (TS-89)
- School Of Wisdom - All 4 Packs/$99 (TS PAK-001)

ORDER TODAY!
www.thewisdomcenter.cc

1-888-WISDOM-1
(1-888-947-3661)

THE WISDOM CENTER • P.O. Box 99 • Denton, Texas 76202

THE WISDOM CENTER

Something incredible is very close to you.

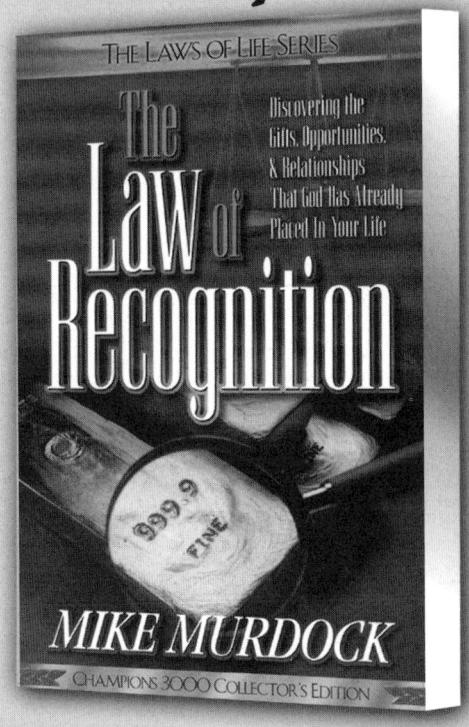

- 47 Keys In RecognizingThe Mate God Has Approved For You
- 14 Facts You Should Know About Your Gifts and Talents
- 17 Important Facts You Should Remember About Your Weakness
- 10 Wisdom Keys That Changed My Life
- 24 Powerful Facts About The Uncommon Dream Within You
- 6 Facts You Should Know About Managing Your Time
- 46 Important Facts You Should Know About Problem Solving

Anything Unrecognized Becomes Uncelebrated. Anything Uncelebrated Becomes Unrewarded. Anything Unrewarded Eventually Exits Your Life. The Law of Recognition can turn a lifetime of failure into instant success. God has provided storehouses of treasures around us and we need only to recognize it. In this teaching you'll learn to recognize the most important gifts in your life.

ORDER TODAY! 1-888-WISDOM-1 (1-888-947-3661)

www.thewisdomcenter.cc

THE WISDOM CENTER • P.O. Box 99 • Denton, Texas 76202

What Matters Most.

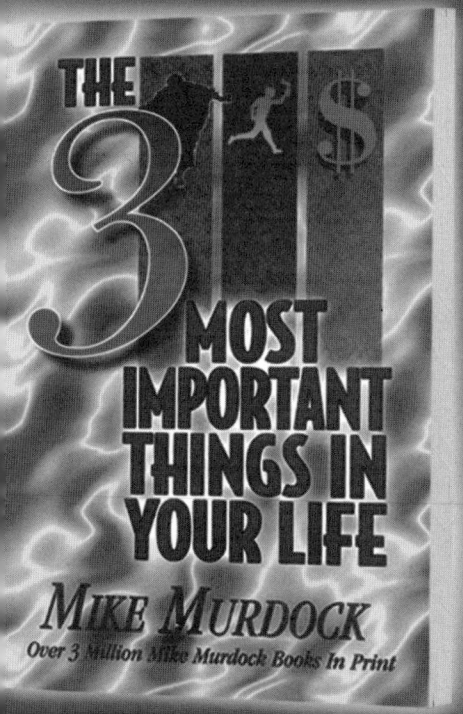

- 17 Facts You Should Know About The Holy Spirit
- The Greatest Weapon The Holy Spirit Has Given You
- 15 Facts About The Love Of The Holy Spirit
- 17 Facts Every Christian Should Know About Grieving The Holy Spirit
- 17 Facts You Should Know About The Anointing
- 3 Ways The Holy Spirit Will Talk To You
- 8 Important Facts About Your Assignment

The Holy Spirit, The Assignment, and The Seed. These three vital areas are the most important things in your life. Mike Murdock addresses each topic in a profound and dynamic way. In this volume he carefully lays out the Wisdom Secrets to Successful living. Your understanding will be energized as knowledge enters your heart and you begin to find your Assignment in the purpose of God. (232 pgs)

Wisdom Is The Principal Thing
Book B-101 / $10
The Wisdom Center

THE WISDOM CENTER

ORDER TODAY!
www.thewisdomcenter.cc

1-888-WISDOM-1
(1-888-947-3661)

THE WISDOM CENTER • P.O. Box 99 • Denton, Texas 76202

The Greatest Secret of the Universe.

- The Holy Spirit and His Greatest Weapon
- The Holy Spirit and Your Prayer Language
- The Holy Spirit and 3 Ways He Speaks To You
- The Holy Spirit As Your Intercessor
- The Holy Spirit and Your Relationships
- The Holy Spirit and Your Assignment
- The Holy Spirit And What Offends Him
- The Holy Spirit And Your Gifts and Talents

The Greatest Secret In The Universe is carefully laid out in this wonderful first volume of the Holy Spirit Handbook. You will discover vital, life-changing facts about your daily companion the Holy Spirit. What Jesus was to the disciples, the Holy Spirit is for us today. Love Him, learn about Him... cherish Him!

Wisdom Is The Principal Thing
Book B-100 / $10
Six Audio Tapes TS-68 / $30
The Wisdom Center

Available also on six tapes for only $30!

ORDER TODAY! 1-888-WISDOM-1 (1-888-947-3661)
www.thewisdomcenter.cc
THE WISDOM CENTER • P.O. Box 99 • Denton, Texas 76202
THE WISDOM CENTER

WISDOM 12 PAK

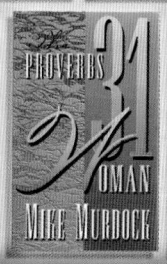

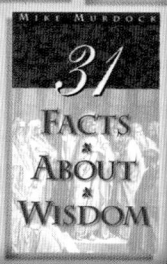

THE MASTER SECRET OF LIFE IS WISDOM

Ignorance Is The Only True Enemy Capable Of Destroying You (Hosea 4:6, Proverbs 11:14)

1.	MY PERSONAL DREAM BOOK	B143	$5.00
2.	THE COVENANT OF FIFTY-EIGHT BLESSINGS	B47	$8.00
3.	WISDOM, GOD'S GOLDEN KEY TO SUCCESS	B71	$7.00
4.	SEEDS OF WISDOM ON THE HOLY SPIRIT	B116	$5.00
5.	SEEDS OF WISDOM ON THE SECRET PLACE	B115	$5.00
6.	SEEDS OF WISDOM ON THE WORD OF GOD	B117	$5.00
7.	SEEDS OF WISDOM ON YOUR ASSIGNMENT	B122	$5.00
8.	SEEDS OF WISDOM ON PROBLEM SOLVING	B118	$5.00
9.	101 WISDOM KEYS	B45	$7.00
10.	31 KEYS TO A NEW BEGINNING	B48	$7.00
11.	THE PROVERBS 31 WOMAN	B49	$7.00
12.	31 FACTS ABOUT WISDOM	B46	$7.00

Wisdom Is The Principal Thing

Book Pak WBL-12 / $30

(A $73 Value!)

The Wisdom Center

THE WISDOM CENTER

ORDER TODAY!

www.thewisdomcenter.cc

1-888-WISDOM-1
(1-888-947-3661)

THE WISDOM CENTER • P.O. Box 99 • Denton, Texas 76202

Money Matters.

This Powerful Video will unleash the Financial Harvest of your lifetime!

VIDEO

31 REASONS PEOPLE DO NOT RECEIVE THEIR FINANCIAL HARVEST

31 REASONS PEOPLE DO NOT RECEIVE THEIR FINANCIAL HARVEST

MIKE MURDOCK

- 8 Scriptural Reasons You Should Pursue Financial Prosperity
- The Secret Prayer Key You Need When Making A Financial Request To God
- The Weapon Of Expectation And The 5 Miracles It Unlocks
- How To Discern Those Who Qualify To Receive Your Financial Assistance
- How To Predict The Miracle Moment God Will Schedule Your Financial Breakthrough

Wisdom Is The Principal Thing

Video VI-17 / $30

Six Audio Tapes / $30 TS-71

Book / $12 B-82

The Wisdom Center

ORDER TODAY!

www.thewisdomcenter.cc

1-888-WISDOM-1
(1-888-947-3661)

THE WISDOM CENTER • P.O. Box 99 • Denton, Texas 76202

The Secret To 1000 Times More.

In this Dynamic Video you will find answers to unleash Financial Flow into your life!

- Habits Of Uncommon Achievers
- The Greatest Success Law I Ever Discovered
- How To Discern Your Place Of Assignment, The Only Place Financial Provision Is Guaranteed
- 3 Secret Keys In Solving Problems For Others
- How To Become The Next Person To Receive A Raise On Your Job

Wisdom Is The Principal Thing
Video VI-16 / $30
Six Audio Tapes / $30 TS-104
Book / $10 B-104
The Wisdom Center

THE WISDOM CENTER

ORDER TODAY!

www.thewisdomcenter.cc

1-888-WISDOM-1
(1-888-947-3661)

THE WISDOM CENTER • P.O. Box 99 • Denton, Texas 76202

Somebody's Future Will Not Begin Until You Enter.

THE ASSIGNMENT:
THE ANOINTING & THE ADVERSITY
MIKE MURDOCK

THE ASSIGNMENT:
THE DREAM & THE DESTINY
MIKE MURDOCK

THE ASSIGNMENT:
THE PAIN & THE PASSION
MIKE MURDOCK

THE ASSIGNMENT:
THE TRIALS & THE TRIUMPHS
MIKE MURDOCK

THIS COLLECTION INCLUDES 4 DIFFERENT BOOKS CONTAINING UNCOMMON WISDOM FOR DISCOVERING YOUR LIFE ASSIGNMENT

- How To Achieve A God-Given Dream And Goal
- How To Know Who Is Assigned To You
- The Purpose And Rewards Of An Enemy

Wisdom Is The Principal Thing
Book Pak WBL-14 / $30
Buy 3-Get 1 Free
($10 Each/$40 Value!)
The Wisdom Center

THE WISDOM CENTER

ORDER TODAY!
www.thewisdomcenter.cc

1-888-WISDOM-1
(1-888-947-3661)

THE WISDOM CENTER • P.O. Box 99 • Denton, Texas 76202

The Secret Place

Library Pak

Songs From The Secret Place

Over 40 Great Songs On 6 Music Tapes
Including "I'm In Love" / Love Songs From The Holy Spirit Birthed In The Secret Place / Side A Is Dr. Mike Murdock Singing / Side B Is Music Only For Your Personal Prayer Time

Seeds Of Wisdom On The Secret Place

4 Secrets The Holy Spirit Reveals In The Secret Place /
The Necessary Ingredients In Creating Your Secret Place /
10 Miracles That Will Happen In The Secret Place

Seeds Of Wisdom On The Holy Spirit

The Protocol For Entering The Presence Of The Holy Spirit /
The Greatest Day Of My Life And What Made It So /
Power Keys For Developing Your Personal Relationship With The Holy Spirit

Wisdom Is The Principal Thing
Book/Tape Pak
SP PAK-001
/ $30
Six Audio Tapes & Two Books
(A $40 Value!)
The Wisdom Center

ORDER TODAY! 1-888-WISDOM-1 (1-888-947-3661)

www.thewisdomcenter.cc

THE WISDOM CENTER • P.O. Box 99 • Denton, Texas 76202

Getting Past The Pain.

- 6 Essential Facts That Must Be Faced When Recovering From Divorce
- 4 Forces That Guarantee Career Success
- 3 Ways Crisis Can Help You
- 4 Reasons You Are Experiencing Opposition To Your Assignment
- How To Predict The 6 Seasons Of Attack On Your Life
- 4 Keys That Can Shorten Your Present Season Of Struggle
- 2 Important Facts You Must Know About Battle & Warfare
- 6 Weapons Satan Uses To Attack Marriages

Wisdom For Crisis Times will give you the answers to the struggle you are facing now, and any struggle you could ever face. Dr. Murdock presents practical steps to help you walk through your "Seasons of Fire."

- 96 Wisdom Keys from God's Word will direct you into the success that God intended for your life. This teaching will unlock the door to your personal happiness, peace of mind, fulfillment and success.

Wisdom Is The Principal Thing
Book B-40 / $9
Six Audio Tapes TS-69 / $30
The Wisdom Center

ORDER TODAY! 1-888-WISDOM-1 (1-888-947-3661)

www.thewisdomcenter.cc

THE WISDOM CENTER • P.O. Box 99 • Denton, Texas 76202

The SCHOOL of WISDOM

- What Attracts Others Toward You
- The Secret Of Multiplying Your Financial Blessings
- What Stops The Flow Of Your Faith
- Why Some Fail And Others Succeed
- How To Discern Your Life Assignment
- How To Create Currents Of Favor With Others
- How To Defeat Loneliness
- 47 Keys In Recognizing The Mate God Has Approved For You
- 14 Facts You Should Know About Your Gifts and Talents
- 17 Important Facts You Should Remember About Your Weakness
- And Much, Much More...

Wisdom Is The Principal Thing

Book/Tape Pak PAK-002 / $30

Six Audio Tapes & Book (A $40 Value!)

The Wisdom Center

ORDER TODAY!

www.thewisdomcenter.cc

1-888-WISDOM-1
(1-888-947-3661)

Learn From The Greatest.

- The Secret Of Handling Rejection
- How To Deal With The Mistakes Of Others
- 5 Power Keys For Effective Delegation To Others
- The Key To Developing Great Faith
- The Greatest Qualities Of Champions
- The Secret Of The Wealthy
- 4 Goal-Setting Techniques
- 10 Facts Jesus Taught About Money

In this dynamic and practical guidebook Mike Murdock points you directly to Jesus, the Ultimate Mentor. You'll take just a moment every day to reflect on His life and actions. And when you do, you'll discover all the key skills and traits that Jesus used... the powerful "leadership secrets" that build true, lasting achievement. Explore them. Study them. Put them to work in your own life and your success will be assured!

Wisdom Is The Principal Thing
Book B-91 / $10
The Wisdom Center

THE WISDOM CENTER

ORDER TODAY!
www.thewisdomcenter.cc

1-888-WISDOM-1
(1-888-947-3661)

THE WISDOM CENTER • P.O. Box 99 • Denton, Texas 76202

Your Rewards In Life Are Determined By The Problems You Solve.

- *3 Simple Ways To Increase Your Income In 90 Days*
- *4 Keys To Recognizing The Problems You Were Created To Solve*
- *12 Rewards Received When You Solve Problems For Others*
- *5 Important Keys To Remember When You Face A Problem*
- *2 Ways You Will Be Remembered*
- *12 Keys to Becoming An Uncommon Problem Solver*
- *6 Keys To Establishing Your Legacy*

ORDER TODAY! **1-888-WISDOM-1 (1-888-947-3661)**

www.thewisdomcenter.cc

THE WISDOM CENTER • P.O. Box 99 • Denton, Texas 76202

You Can Have It.

- Why Sickness Is Not The Will Of God
- How To Release The Powerful Forces That Guarantee Blessing
- The Incredible Role Of Your Memory And The Imagination
- The Hidden Power Of Imagination And How To Use It Properly
- The Difference Between The Love Of God And His Blessings
- 3 Steps In Increasing Your Faith
- 2 Rewards That Come When You Use Your Faith In God
- 7 Powerful Keys Concerning Your Faith

Dreams and desires begin as photographs within our hearts and minds - things that we want to happen in our future. God plants these pictures as invisible Seeds within us. God begins every miracle in your life with a Seed-picture... the invisible idea that gives birth to a visible blessing. In this teaching, you will discover your desires and how to concentrate on watering and nurturing the growth of your Dream-Seeds until you attain your God-given goals.

Wisdom Is The Principal Thing
Book B-11 / $9
Six Audio Tapes TS-2 / $30
The Wisdom Center

ORDER TODAY!
www.thewisdomcenter.cc

1-888-WISDOM-1
(1-888-947-3661)

THE WISDOM CENTER • P.O. Box 99 • Denton, Texas 76202

Where You Are Determines What Grows In You.

- 4 Secrets The Holy Spirit Reveals In The Secret Place
- Master Keys In Cultivating An Effective Prayer Life
- The Necessary Ingredients In Creating Your Secret Place
- 10 Miracles That Will Happen In The Secret Place

Wisdom Is The Principal Thing

Book B-115 / $5

The Wisdom Center

THE WISDOM CENTER

ORDER TODAY! **1-888-WISDOM-1 (1-888-947-3661)**

www.thewisdomcenter.cc

THE WISDOM CENTER • P.O. Box 99 • Denton, Texas 76202

Run To Win.

- 10 Ingredients For Success
- 10 Lies Many People Believe About Money
- 20 Keys For Winning At Work
- 20 Keys To A Better Marriage
- 3 Facts Every Parent Should Remember
- 5 Steps Out Of Depression
- The Greatest Wisdom Principle I Ever Learned
- 7 Keys To Answered Prayer
- God's Master Golden Key To Total Success
- The Key To Understanding Life

Everyone needs to feel they have achieved something with their life. When we stop producing, loneliness and laziness will choke all enthusiasm from our living. What would you like to be doing? What are you doing about it? Get started on a project in your life. Start building on your dreams. Resist those who would control and change your personal goals. Get going with this powerful teaching and reach your life goals!

Wisdom Is The Principal Thing
Book B-01 / $10
Six Audio Tapes TS-01 / $30
The Wisdom Center

ORDER TODAY!

www.thewisdomcenter.cc

1-888-WISDOM-1
(1-888-947-3661)

THE WISDOM CENTER • P.O. Box 99 • Denton, Texas 76202

THE SECRET.

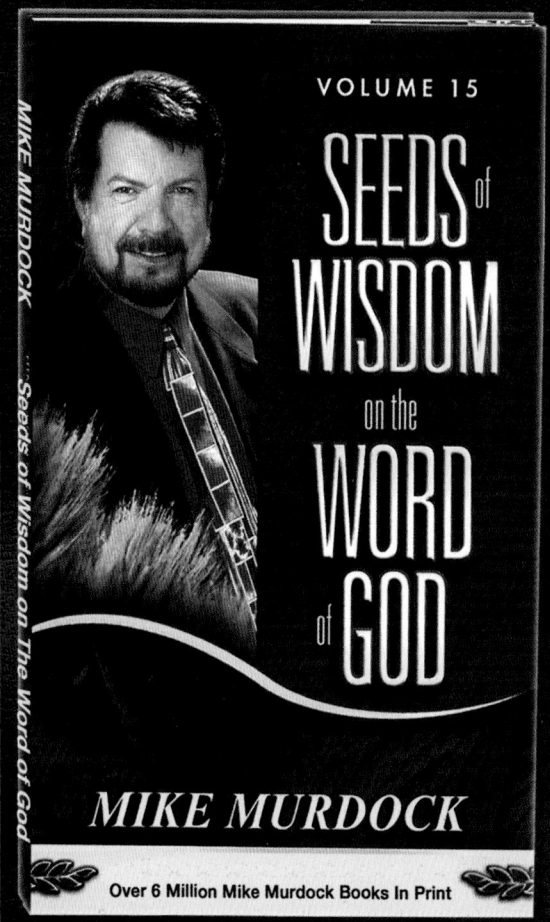

- 11 Reasons Why The Bible Is The Most Important Book On Earth
- 12 Problems The Word Of God Can Solve In Your Life
- 4 Of My Personal Bible Reading Secrets
- 4 Steps To Building A Spiritual Home
- 9 Wisdom Keys To Being Successful In Developing The Habit Of Reading The Word Of God

Wisdom Is The Principal Thing

Book B-117 / $5

The Wisdom Center

THE WISDOM CENTER

ORDER TODAY! **1-888-WISDOM-1 (1-888-947-3661)**

www.thewisdomcenter.cc

THE WISDOM CENTER • P.O. Box 99 • Denton, Texas 76202

Assignment

Your Assignment Is Your Discovery, Not Your Decision.

VOLUME 20

SEEDS of WISDOM on YOUR ASSIGNMENT

MIKE MURDOCK

Over 6 Million Mike Murdock Books In Print

- 11 Seasons Of Preparation For Your Assignment
- 6 Rewards Of Pain
- 6 Keys For Developing An Obsession For Your Assignment
- 3 Wisdom Keys To Turning Your Anger Into Passion For Your Assignment

Wisdom Is The Principal Thing

Book B-122 / $5

The Wisdom Center

THE WISDOM CENTER

ORDER TODAY!

www.thewisdomcenter.cc

1-888-WISDOM-1
(1-888-947-3661)

THE WISDOM CENTER • P.O. Box 99 • Denton, Texas 76202

WISDOM COLLECTION

8

SECRETS OF THE UNCOMMON MILLIONAIRE

1. The Uncommon Millionaire Conference Vol. 1 (Six Cassettes)
2. The Uncommon Millionaire Conference Vol. 2 (Six Cassettes)
3. The Uncommon Millionaire Conference Vol. 3 (Six Cassettes)
4. The Uncommon Millionaire Conference Vol. 4 (Six Cassettes)
5. 31 Reasons People Do Not Receive Their Financial Harvest (256 Page Book)
6. Secrets of the Richest Man Who Ever Lived (178 Page Book)
7. 12 Seeds Of Wisdom Books On 12 Topics
8. The Gift Of Wisdom For Leaders Desk Calendar
9. 101 Wisdom Keys On Tape (Audio Tape)
10. In Honor Of The Holy Spirit (Music Cassette)
11. 365 Memorization Scriptures On The Word Of God (Audio Cassette)

Wisdom Is The Principal Thing

THE WISDOM COLLECTION 8
SECRETS OF THE UNCOMMON MILLIONAIRE

WC-08 /$195

The Wisdom Center

THE WISDOM CENTER

ORDER TODAY! 1-888-WISDOM-1 (1-888-947-3661)

www.thewisdomcenter.cc

The Secrets For Surviving.

How To Get Through The Storms Of Your Life!

Avoiding the #1 Trap Satan Uses Against Believers!

Keys To Discovering Wrong People In Your Life!

Satan's 3 Most Effective Weapons!

How To Use Adversity As A Stepping Stone To Wisdom!

How To Stand When Everything Is Falling Apart!

7 Seasons Satan Always Attacks You!

Battle Techniques Of War-Weary Saints!

Reversing Satanic Strategy!

How To Get Back Up When The Devil Puts You Down!

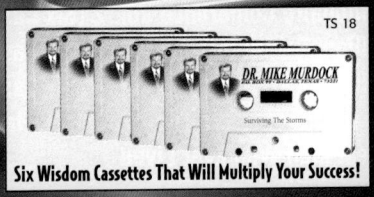

Six Wisdom Cassettes That Will Multiply Your Success!

This life changing and revolutionary teaching is based on the Wisdom and The Principles of other champions in the Word of God. You will discover the greatest Wisdom Keys on earth and will begin unlocking the treasure containing every desired gift and miracle you are pursuing.

Wisdom Is The Principal Thing

Tape Pak TS-18 / $30

Six Audio Tapes

The Wisdom Center

THE WISDOM CENTER

ORDER TODAY!

www.thewisdomcenter.cc

1-888-WISDOM-1
(1-888-947-3661)

THE WISDOM CENTER • P.O. Box 99 • Denton, Texas 76202